What rich people are hiding from you?

There are no magic words for success, but there are free golden keys to open the success doors and that you are able to get them easily if you want.

Welcome dear reader

Hope you'll enjoy while learn something new

Big thanks to all people that inspired me to write this book.

Thanks to my friends, my clients, and all people I deal with in daily basis for their advices, and for their willing to test the different aspects of life to may not only judge by themselves, but also to give a clear feedback and advices to other people.

I am taking also this opportunity to thank my dear mom, and my dear wife for the effort they are doing to give me time, needed support, and high motivation dose to step forward each day.

Before starting: This book is a result of multiple projects and deals, and not an ordinary story.

Please be sure to give time and focus to the coming points so not only to enjoy the reading, but to understand as much as possible, and be able to start a project for your own.

First advice: "IF YOU WANT TO SUCCEED START DOING IT AND STOP DREAMING ABOUT IT".

Summary

Introduction

Many rich people are hiding some secret projects and businesses management strategies ideas and skills.

In many cases, some rich people got like so using simple and low cost ideas that made them jump up from "0" to "billions of dollars", while other people were wondering how they did it? Was it a chance or a smart move? Was it a risk taking spirit or some stupid adventure that turned for real? And, why they had that much luck with their projects?

What I need you to be sure of is that luck is a factor, yes it is, "BUT" when the ideas are smartly calculated and well based.

Money is there but it will not wait for you if you don't step forward to it, and here is what this book is for, to show you how rich people did to get rich, and how the majority of them are doing to keep climbing the money mountain.

There are many ways you can start your own business in a legal way, structured way, and a vision in time of what you can reach and what is next step.

So, are you ready to open your mind and start walking into your way to be a business owner? if you are then let's start.

The themes we will describe to you are the following:

- o Things you have to know about rich people
- o Strategies to be successful
- o Advice to get rich

Hope you a good reading

Things you have to know about rich people

Rich people are not all that much smart, because being smart is not a success rule as much as being able to plan, to study eventualities, evaluate risks and benefits at short and long terms.

What you need to be sure of, is that rich business people are doing some basic things that are accessible for everyone, but are used differently to serve in reaching each one final goals. So if you didn't pay attention to the word I will mention it again: "BASIC", this word is the key to success, don't complicate your life by searching for some kind of magic words or ritual to change your life, and don't think that making money is as hard as reaching the sky, if you believe in yourself, and read what's coming carefully, you'll be able to go to the next step and start making money. ("I believe that you are already in your 1st step while you are reading this business starting keys revelation").

What are those basic thing? Here are they:

1. Education
2. Legal Business
3. Money making strategy

NB: For the keys 1 and 3, the order can be swiped for some cases, but once you start your own work, you must review them again and again each period so you keep improving your skills, and your clients' satisfaction.

Don't imagine you know these points, believe that your ideas will be shuffled and your knowledge renewed when you will know that rich people aren't stopping learning in such way to be able to review their strategies over and over again. And here we are describing each point's aspects and methods, as well as how you can benefit from it as "they do".

Education

Education means feeding your mind and body with new knowledge, skills, experiences, that you or anyone from your family or your work team can benefit from. The majority of people think that to learn they must go to schools or universities, which is right but is just one of an endless count of learning ways.

To be successful in your learning you must think about the following:

a. Define your business type and if needed the headcount of your team.
b. Create a list of needed knowledge and skills to succeed in your project.
c. Find the source of each type of knowledge: here you'll have different categories of sources:
    - Schools
    - Experienced people
    - Seminars
    - Consultants
    - Family old people and friends (good friend): because they might know people that tried or succeeded in similar projects but in different ways.
    - Business management books
    - ....
d. Put the skills according to categories in a table, and start calculating the cost to learn each knowledge or skill separately and in groups if possible to lower the cost and learn as much as possible.
e. Put the charges of your education program on your business budgets: you must have at least three budgets, short term budget, long term budget, and emergency budget.
f. Start learning the free skills first, at least till you start earning enough to teach yourself payed ones.
g. Practice

The list above is not a long one compared to what others do, and you need to run it in a periodic cycle mode to evaluate what was beneficial, and what wasn't so you can learn more, save more, and expand your business network more and more.

The magic takes place when you configure all these points on what your actual and future customers will need to have in your product, and what is the most accurate process to manufacture theses needs, and introduce them to customers in an excellent way.

Cote: Customers pay for what they need less, and more for what you need. If you don't sell both, you lose.

Now, what are the things that successful business men and women started learning first? and what they keep learning every day?

The below list is will blow your mind if you read it carefully:

1. What are the things that successful business men and women started learning first?

   - Market study
   - Budgeting
   - Brand creation
   - Advertising
   - Added value creation
   - Market repartition strategies
   - Competition and association
   - Customers categories
   - …

   The list doesn't stop here but I'm giving you the top 8 things to start with and which I gave as advice to many people that had big results by going through.

2. What they keep learning every day?

   - Market expansion strategies
   - Market repartition strategies
   - Stock repartition and balancing
   - Liquidity management
   - Budgeting and charges balancing
   - Automation of purchasing and selling processes
   - Marketing and advertising
   - Sponsoring
   - …

   Read carefully the list as the keys to success are here given without schooling, just search them on any platform and start your journey of learning.

Both lists can be learned for free, you can google them, be present into seminars, as specialists, by books and learn by yourself…

But the most important is your will to learn, and to take you time to understand and practice, you must not be in hurry, you must be in hunger.

The first lever is explained and shortly walked as I don't want to put you in a labyrinth of words. I want you to get the keys of success directly, and what I'm sure of is that people who will read this book will search for more explanations, you will find some, but what you don't find you need to search for.

I'm initiating your learning process here and now, and give you a push, think about the lists you were reading before and ask yourself: did someone told you about these lists? Were you aware about the points mentioned in?

Sure that you'll tell yourself that no, I wasn't aware and no one told me, but now I know, I "learned" what I have to search for, and this is the first step in my learning journey.

So what you think is mandatory as knowledge and skills to manage well your project is now clear if not totally changed, learned something from the previous pages, and you must plan your education program, but don't rush yourself, and just start with the basics.

One more free advice for you is to not believe social media and news programs about market evolution, don't listen too much, make your own search, and see for yourself in exchange stocks, international products markets, popular companies' successes and failures: how they achieved, and how they managed priorities, and successful YOUNG people that started from nothing to billions (they are the teachers in our era, they are bad teachers in some cases as they don't reveal their real success keys, but even so you can learn something from their stories), and don't be dreamers who listen to motivational stories and wish to succeed the same way, be doers who pass to action to succeed in your own way.

Legal Business

Is it possible to work in a legal mode and get rich?

Yes, it is, even in drugs manufacturing you can be working according law if your products are for medication manufacturing purpose, and you are authorized by the government.

Success is not based or related to drugs dealing, weapons dealing, or any bad kind of dark blood businesses as a lot of people do think and imagine. Many are thinking the rich people would not make it if they didn't deal with some suspicious business, and this is not true.

In fact, the great known successful billionaires (sorry for not giving names by the way as it's not our goal) are dealing with constructions, high tech, petroleum, air transportation, shipping, banking, education, consulting, pharmaceutical industry, automotive industry, restaurants, fishing, clothing, shoes, and other thousands activities.

I'm telling you this to push you another step in your path, your idea may be a new market category in the future, but do you want to be the owner of the idea but without benefit, or you want to have a part from the market with a revenue that jumps in your pocket each time your idea is sold.

Now how can you work legally in those legal categories? How can you build your business without thinking that one day someone will knock your door and arrest you or take your fortune away? The answer is simple: get things on papers, get authorizations and get a clear situation with your government and your bank, pay your taxes in time, focus on details and deadlines, don't rush but don't lose time.

One thing to be sure of is that every government is checking his citizens' fortunes evolution, and at a certain time they will ask you what are you doing and from where do you get your money? And to save time and answer this question before you get it asked, get in touch with your bank once your project start getting benefits.

Banks are a kind of special agents working for the government, and that known, you don't need to lose time explaining while your money and business are on hold, it will be better to clarify everything to your bank before your first money transfer to your account.

Do you understand? If not re-read the previous 3 paragraphs.

The second main question is how to guaranty the continuity of your business (in legal mode)?

The answer is simple, but hard to achieve: you have to get things done by yourself and don't wait for anyone to help or to take care of any task without supervising him and ensuring the quick and accurate reaction to solve problems and achieve your project first phases in time.

Each project owner must:

- Make the planning according to budget, product development needed time, advertising methods and modes, markets locations, and customer background…

- Don't under estimate the value of any detail.
- Supervise and be the first one to assure the responsibility of getting things done correctly.
- Ensure a situation with governing laws.
- Ensure the good practices: no bribe money is given or taken from any part.
- Respect of employees to rules. Each bad mentality need to be excluded.
- Get advices from an experienced lawyer.
- Pay taxes in time, and motivate your employees.
- Import/Export products from/to trusted and certified contacts.
- Ensure the positive feedbacks and the satisfaction of customers: this will make your brand star shine more and more.
- Pay the total of your bank credit amount ASAP: this will be the first thing to think about once you start earning money: banks care for their benefits, not for yours, so once you start getting money in your pocket start saving it, and when you get all the money needed to pay your credit do it without hesitation as you will always be winner in all cases.
- Don't trust anyone that comes after you start your project and ask you to be part of your team, the good ones join you and motivate you to begin and so they deserve to be part of your team: yes, it's a hard world out there, so sometimes you need to be hard too.
- Avoid haters and bribe askers, and surround yourself with honest people and contacts.

The points above include some working keys to use in your legal business growth management, while other points are more related to how your personality should be forged.

Don't hesitate to reject any bad practice, or person, focus on your success but don't be a fool.

Don't hesitate to ask for advice and help from experienced people, but don't pay for illegal services.

Haters and jealous people are without importance if your work is far from their reach. The big fishes (important adversaries) in the market are important, they must be known, and separated strategies must be implemented to counter their strikes, or to invite them to beneficial collaborations.

Taxes payment is the mirror that reflect your honesty and business growth/stability trend and motivate your government/Banks to support you in case of crisis.

Your products descriptions must contain all details about composition and possible effects on customers, as well as the authorization to produce them and certification (serials / Logos).

Money making

Assuming you have done all what was described in the previous pages and more, and now your project is implemented, the real work start now, the moment of truth is close and you are worried about success and failure, you have many storms playing with your mind and many things to take care of.

You are wondering how the successful rich people can calm their mind storm, and get focused? How can they control all what surround them? And what do they do to make the money work for them?

Consider that all projects are managed according to standard basics, and to few personalized parameters. This being told, you must understand the following:

1. As any project, yours have an Input and an Output:

   - During your project study, you have identified your input elements, the source of, and the frequency of acquisition: so, all you need is to establish the system to manage that by yourself or by competent person. Define the physical store location and the structure of your input, an inventory frequency, and a clear database to follow the consumption of your stock, and the supplies deliveries to it.

   - Output: create a follow-up of you customers. Put in graphs your sales to identify the top demanded products, the top customers' categories (age, life style, intellectual background…), the top customers' regions, and so on...
   This will allow you to identify the products that don't sell as wanted, so you can change your strategy of presenting, advertising, or market orientation.

2. Establish a ramp-up plan, in which you'll work on the previous points, and you'll be able to identify the potential and occurring wastes.
The wastes need to be eliminated as they are part of the money that have to go to your pocket, not to scrap.
Wastes can be: unneeded material or equipment, people, empty spaces, big stocks, ...: think lean.

3. Take care of your suppliers:

   - Check the suppliers' situation in the market: are they growing or are they dropping due to some kind of issues. You need to follow-up your suppliers closely to don't get bad surprises like raises in prices, variation of the quality of supplies, overdue deliveries, or stopped deliveries...

   - Get strong relation with your suppliers if you have any, and be a source of motivation more than being just a demanding customer, push them to improve and don't accept illogical explanations for any failure to the contract conditions.

   - Pay your suppliers in time.

   - Check out their capacity evolution so you can benefit from it in the future if you plan to enlarge your business market.

   - Be careful and make sure that any new agreement is documented

4. Take care of your customers:

   - Follow-up your customers' satisfaction, and give persuasive solution to any claimed issue.

   - Communicate with them, and keep them always informed about your new products: easy and free advertising.

   - If your customers are enterprises, you need to keep an eye on their evolution and capacity, to take profit from their growth and grow with them, or to plan and check for other customers to attract.

   - Get paid for your products and services in time.

- Any new requirement from a customer need to be documented and the cost behind need to be calculated, negotiated and added to the product price.

- Ask and encourage your customers (if they are individuals) for free advertising, and be sure that there are thousands of ways to do that politely and legally, just keep in mind that a happy satisfied customer can attract another 20 new ones "at least".

5. Take care of your team: if you are not alone in your project, then:

  - Coach your team and guide them to the main goal.

  - Ensure the communication tools are available to avoid stress and time loss.

  - Balance the tasks repartition.

  - Follow-up the performance of each member and motivate them to improve.

  - Run through details and don't wait for explanations: being aware of what is happening will help you and your team to react in time before the occurrence of any inconveniences.

  - Avoid stressing work atmosphere: better will be to have a motivating work place.

  - ……..

6. Take care of yourself:

  - Fix your charges for planned periods: this will allow you to estimate your gains and will make the follow-up of achievements easier.

  - For each product or pack of products sold, separate gains from charges.

- Start saving money to may be able to pay bank credit if you have any. Also, to may at a certain time make another step and invest in a new project or extend the one you have: here the money will start working for you.

- If you don't have your own house then by one, and avoid renting. The house will not only be yours, but consider it also as a money store that can be used later if anything bad happens. And consider the rent cost as an extra charge that need to be avoided.

- Don't hurry on buying a personal care, instead, let it be a business car with your brand, products/services list, and contacts on it.

- Help others, but don't waste your time and your money.

The successful people do have hearts and emotions like all human, but they developed, each one by his own methods, an emotional intelligence that keep them focus on what is more important on their life: "SUCCESS" and a better life.

They are not arrogant (not all), but they must be serious and logical.

As a future successful person you must instruct yourself to avoid being trapped by your emotions, and fix a key idea in your mind: "You must ensure a better life for you and your family, you can be generous but not a wasteful or a fool, you can have friends, but don't let them access to your work secrets"

If making money is hard, losing it is very easy.

The ones that underestimated you before, don't deserve to be in your network later.

Don't seek others admiration or valuing you at your worth, this is achieved automatically once you succeed.

Be close, but hard to reach: define some redlines and rules that will guaranty the respect of your privet personal and professional life.

2 Strategies to use to be successful

Since you are now aware about what do the actual rich people think like, and act like, and manage their business like, you are asking yourself what the most accurate strategy or strategies to adopt in the future.

Here I will give you 3 free and not common strategies that will blow your mind and help you in your success pursuit.

Expand your network

Once you have defined what your product/service will be, you must promote and advertise it, of course, in the beginning you'll need some people to test and review your products/services.

> ❖ Using the free method: Based only on your effort.

As everyone will think, you'll share the information with your network, and here comes the necessity of having a network that includes potential customers, not only family and friends. You must reach people from different categories and regions, even with different ideologies and backgrounds.

Take your time to design a good product or service ID/LOGO and presentation, list it's benefits, what you are promising and what you are committed to do for your future customer (think about bundled offers, competitive prices, guaranties, assistance of customers for free or for low prices, …).

You need to make sure that what you are offering will attract as much as possible of people and push those people to transmit your offers to others (free advertising).

Each person you interact with must be listed, identified, and evaluated in such way to focus on what matter. the ranking can like below:

> ➤ Motivated to purchase.
> ➤ Motivated to transmit the information to other.

➢ Both preview descriptions.
➢ Not motivated at all

This will allow you to create a certain population that will be waiting for the release of your product and will ensure you to get the needed first push to your business in term of sales and positive reviews.

❖ Using the paid method: Based on your effort and money.

When you have done all what is in your power to reach as mush as possible of potential customers, you need to take other methods into consideration, especially paid advertising.

The ways to do that are many and easy, you can do it on some social media advertising modes, or you can ask another person that have an important number of followers to support you and inform his network about you and your brand.

This method requires the estimation of how much you can invest on advertising to reach people. Many social media sites give you the opportunity to advertise for your product with the possibility to define the period of advertising, the area in which you want to advertise, what is the kind of your advertising (Video, link, presentation,…), and costs categories depending on those parameters.

To note that most investor think that they will lose the money allowed to advertising, while this is a wrong idea, it is too cheap compared the number of customer that can by your products later, it's cheap if compared to the cost needed to reach each one separately, it's really cheap.

But you need to understand that the rule is valid even after you start selling and when you think you have a stable customers platform. Nothing is stable, and also, there more than 7 billion humans on earth that can be your customers, so don't be satisfied by a certain result, and try to expand your network to get your part from this huge cake.

Planning projects by customers categories

As already said, and during the advertising to your product, you'll be aiming to attract a certain category of customers for each product, then if you have multiple products, you need to have a clear repartition of customers with a detailed description.

Knowing who are your customers, where do they live, what are their incomes averages, what are their intellectual backgrounds, what are their believes and religions, will help you in setting you commercialization parameters, as well as logical prices.

From a customer satisfaction point of view, you must focus on:

- What do the customer need to have as a product: Design, effect, price, delivery date, result, guaranty of the result for an acceptable time term.

- What will motivate your customer to purchase other products: satisfaction from the first product use, good presented invitation to use other products, bundle of products with low cost and good quality, positive review and opinions from other users, hospitality and after sale support.

- What are the customer suggestions and requirement: design improvement, final result, low cost, support and indications.

Then you can review your projects according to interested customers, implement possible improvements, invite customers to test the new upgraded products, take their feedbacks to commercialize your products in other/new categories to increase the trust in your mark and be able to expand your market share.

By identifying the customers categories and defining which products are suitable for each category with a suitable and admissible price, you can easily monitor your gains trend even in matter of time : some products sell more in a certain season of the year, while the sales can drop in other period of the year, so you have to identify these products and plan the cycle of your products advertising or new products launch time.

Also, identifying which people are more active by season, and how much they can spend in each season.

Successful businesswomen and businessmen are so because they care about all details, an keep their eyes wide open to detect any change or trend. For so you have to learn to give each detail the needed analysis and a specific reaction mode.

Advices to follow your projects evolution efficiently:

1. Put all data in a dynamic database

2. Monitor it frequently if not daily

3. Define your emergency plan to avoid any issues or claims

4. Define your reaction modes to any situation

5. Follow-up your suppliers

6. Follow-up the performance of your team

7. Analyze details

8. Motivate your customers

9. Keep an eye on your market share % evolution

10. Keep an eye on the competitors

11. Don't stop improving

12. When you are stressed, calm down, ask for advices, and don't rush on taking decisions.

My advices to become rich

Test what you are thinking about

Success is not result of theories and estimations, but it is resulting from testing those theories and estimation many times over and over, and learning from your errors each time.

Be aware of the risks behind your testing and practicing, don't neglect anything and don't let things to luck, but don't hope to succeed if don't make some mistakes.

Mistakes will make aware of them on of how to avoid them later in other projects. Also, no baby is making the first step without falling many time before. So business baby, how will you walk without falling?

Ask yourself this question, and read again the previous pages for answers.

Don't start more than 2 projects per time

If you are for your own or with a team, I'll advise you to start only **one** project at the beginning till having it running by itself in approximately 80%, then invest your time and effort in a second one.

Later when you have good running project(s), you'll want to launch other subprojects also (I mean by subprojects the ones that have an activity that is related 100% to the main project: like an externalization of some tasks for more efficiency in your processes...): for those, don't launch more than **2** each time as they will require a lot of effort to be managed and controlled, and there can be big risks on the main project stability.

Conclusion

There is nothing hard in the life of successful people as the effort they are dedicating to their business worth it.

Hard is the description of the life of the ones that are trapped a cycle that never ends, the ones that one day will open their eyes and ask themselves: how did I got old? And why didn't I change my life when others did?

Ask yourself where you want to be after 10 years from now?

Act while you still have time, and each day ask yourself what will you do tomorrow?